Watching Whales

W9-AXP-702

Contents

Brenda Parkes

Introduction

Once, whales were hunted for their meat, blubber, and bones. But now it is against the law to hunt most whales.

Today, scientists and other people watch whales. They have found out many interesting things about how these animals live in the sea.

How Whales Breathe

Whales live in the sea, but they are not fish. When whales are under the water they hold their breath.

When they come up out of the water they breathe out. Spouts of moist air shoot up into the air.

Different Kinds of Whales

There are many kinds of whales. Some whales have teeth. They are called toothed whales.

Other kinds of whales do not have teeth.
They are called baleen whales. They have baleen
plates that help them eat. Baleen plates keep
small fish and plants in the whale's mouth and
help strain food out of the water.

Studying Humpbacks

One kind of baleen whale that scientists like to watch is the humpback.

Like all whales, humpbacks have two tail fins called flukes.

Their flukes have markings that are like fingerprints in people. No two humpbacks have the same markings.

Singing Whales

Humpbacks can sing. Each of their songs is made up of a series of sounds that repeat. Their songs can go on for hours.

Some scientists have recorded humpback songs. They think that humpbacks sing to attract a mate or warn off enemies.

At Home in the Sea

When it is summer, humpbacks live and feed in cold waters. They sometimes use special tricks to catch fish. The whale can dive down and blow bubbles. These bubbles act like a net and trap lots of little fish.

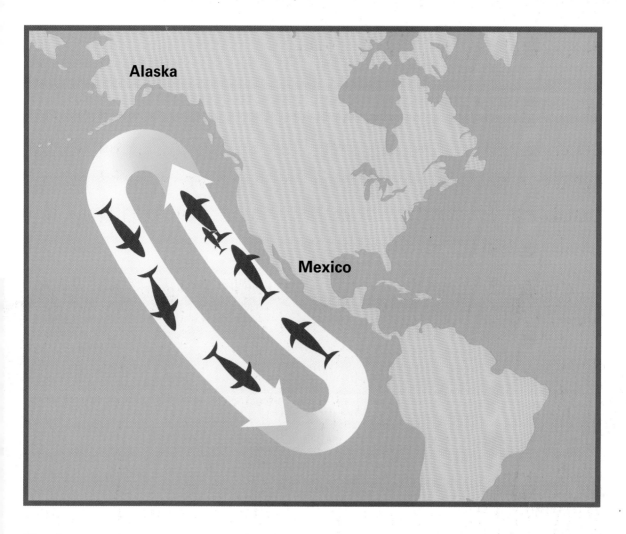

Before the winter comes, the whales travel, or migrate, to warmer oceans. The arrows on this map show one migration route. Each summer these whales live in the cold waters near Alaska. Each winter they travel south to live in the warm waters near Mexico.

Baby Whales

Baby whales are called calves. Humpback calves are born after the mother whales arrive in the warmer waters. When a calf is born, its mother helps it to the surface. Then the new baby takes its first breath.

Adult humpbacks do not eat while they are in warm waters. But the calves feed on their mothers' milk. When the calves are strong enough, the whales migrate back to their cold-water feeding ground.

These people are whale watching. Someday you may see a whale up close, too.